DOOR UPON DOOR

ANNEMARIE AUSTIN

Door upon Door

BLOODAXE BOOKS

ISBN: 1 85224 459 3

First published 1999 by
Bloodaxe Books Ltd,
P.O. Box 1SN,
Newcastle upon Tyne NE99 1SN.

Bloodaxe Books Ltd acknowledges
the financial assistance of Northern Arts.

Cover printing by J. Thomson Colour Printers Ltd, Glasgow.

Printed in Great Britain by
Cromwell Press Ltd, Trowbridge, Wiltshire.

for my father
these poems
some of which are his already

Acknowledgements

Acknowledgements are due to the editors of the following publications where some of these poems first appeared: *Agenda*, *Ambit*, *Blade*, Housman Society centenary poetry anthology (1996), *Interactions*, *London Magazine*, *Modern Painters*, *New Statesman & Society*, *New Welsh Reriew*, *The North*, *Outposts*, *Poetry and Audience*, *Poetry Review*, *Poetry Wales*, *Reflecting Families: An Anthology of Poems* (BBC Educational, 1995), *Seam*, *Smiths Knoll*, *Southfields*, *Stand*, *Thumbscrew*, *The Times Literary Supplement* and *Writing Women*.

Contents

The Indigo Bedspread

1

It is terrible as an army with banners because
she saw it worn, trailed across the carpet
by another, palpably naked at knee and shoulder,
when he stood at the door and for the first time
did not let her in.
                    Then behind him in the hallway
the indigo bedspread for a meagre robe around
the unknown pale-armed woman who showed
herself to be at home.
                    The indigo bedspread she
had lain under over and over with him, now
a train behind small bare heels, a makeshift
kimono on a woman roused from sleep. Bundled
together at the breasts, parting halfway along
the thighs, following those feet through the passage.

2

Make it go away – as if it were indeed a banner,
tattered after battle, stained with famous blood
and put to rest in the side aisle of a church
where it will safely fade over the centuries,
turn to a dust-grey net.
                    Fold it as origami into
an awkward bird and let it loose from the attic
over London and the river. Hear it flap and
creak above and make a big shadow on the road
like a cloud before the sun. Watch it grow small
very slowly as a flying swan does. See it pass.

3

At first the indigo rubbed off on clean sheets
and on her hands shading them oddly. They
thought they might turn into Tuareg people
rolled only in its folds on a summer night.

The woman had white inside arms where her skin
touched the bunched cloth. No dark tidemark
slanted above her knees or at her armpits.
They had worn the dye off on their bodies
long before her.

     Make it go away. See it pass.

Watershed

I read about the centenarian woman potter
whose work – she said – continued as distraction
from too much thinking about young men.

It does not go away then – the sensual mental walk
up the inside curve of an arm, or the wish to press
the open mouth against a breastbone thinly dressed
in skin, a longing to lie again in an embrace's cradle?

But what young man will think in an equivalent way
of the old woman bent above the potter's wheel,
or me, now at the watershed, seeing my once-smooth skin
begin its tiny pleating over and back from the bone?

I consider the future beyond the crest of this hill
with its downslope into solitude, where my flesh
will heal more slowly, where the ache of the phantom
of this amputation will keep me awake at night...

Though only alone was I ever graced by such as
that mole's sudden eruption a yard from my foot
when I sat and read in a drought-ridden garden –
and with such a live racket of tearing roots and
stems, such a commotion of insects in the grass...

Marriage

How unlike they were –
each what the other was not –
the earth and air;

and the border between
clear in that flat space
of drought-browned lawn;

when what was of the earth
thrust up into the air
making a new relation.

I saw the throbbing
in a patch of grass,
heard the tearing

such as cattle make
wrapping their tongues
round the green blades

and breaking them;
then the mole hit the light,
came from the ground erect.

It was all alive:
quivering sometimes
like a dog shaking dry;

driving blindly forward
like a small machine
in velvet; furrowing

the flattened dry lawn
to wake tremors
of insects crawling.

And this was an earth creature –
out of supposedly
solid, wet and cold –

which had not only
disarrayed the light,
but broken the ground open

so that its honeycombing
threaded with air
the idea of underfoot.

Revenants

He had tried to block their nest under the garden step,
but the wasps at once unpicked the wet cement and kept
their way to the brood-cells open.
                     Later, the day when,
rising in the dark, he let electric yellow light
spill out into the glassed-in porch and watched
its space fill up with greyish wasps, ghostly
against the glass but loud and growing louder.

He heard of the bees' nest melted out of a chimney,
how honey had poured into the hearth and smoke-entangled
bees were gathered from the fireplace in plastic
bin-bags that squirmed and pulsed and buzzed.

When winter arrived and he blocked the nest again,
he was sure that the wasps were sleeping but would come
digging their way up through the lawn to find him.

Foreground

The dead speak up
from little beds
in their little rooms,
voices like grasshoppers' –
stridulent background.
Once in a while
the mind lets them through,
the dead become foreground.

The great insect eye
looks into mine –
grasshopper on my chest;
weight hardly there,
but palpable.
Regard of a dead woman
in the half-dark.

She has changed underground,
struggling through
egg cases, pupae.
She is tinged with earth's sepia,
shrunk by its liquids;
still she leans on my ribs
and her eye is close to mine.
(Brown, knowing gaze –
though her iris
alive was blue.)

The dead woman–grasshopper
made her nest
in the straw coils
of my skull box,
she whispers to
the inside of the ear.

I am not at all in love
with the dry, interior voice,
its sawing, its same call,
dictation repeated, repeated.
Yet I move to the head note...
A brown and shrunken creature
creeps rustling
through cranium halls,
contuses my lawless heart
with her small dessicated claw.

My ambit is like a graveyard:
grass growing up and up,
ivy submerging headstones,
root tendrils lifting, tipping
walls of a mausoleum
where
in an August blaze
it strikes up –
the sawn background –
I hear
through waves of haze
dead voices
coming forward.

The Sand Spring

It was not here yesterday – this cup of water
with the restless cloud of sand at work
within; there was no channel,
cutting the beach in two curves,
before small runnels spreading
in the shape of a half-closed fan...

Nor was there this memory, welling up
into a different life... It rained last night
to feed the spring. I taste its water
on my finger – sweetly bland,
unsalted by the dunes... We came here often
in late evening, talked in the car in the dark.

Through the summer and into autumn,
growing colder. My head on his shoulder
over the gap of the gears. Years ago...
Children are digging new channels in the sand
and dam the old one. Dogs wade and drink.
The fan spreads or shrinks, its pattern shifting.

I remember a river heading for the sea
that stopped instead in a spoon-shaped pool,
ten feet of shingle bank between it
and the waves. Weed clotted there...
Memory hoards its unfinished business.
The pool seeped underground to underwater.

Under Glass

If Kristallnacht could be undone –
film run in reverse – it would build
to this glass bell above the ghetto
cemetery, the seven synagogues:
Jehovah's wax fruit or trophy
songbirds with vitreous eyes
to spark light through the dusk.

In fact the fruit has dropped across
the path, wasps ride its cider
fumes between the tombstones,
my foot prints its brown snow-slush.
The names on the graves do not correspond
to anybody, any body, underneath them,
though those markers are true records.

This is a photograph made from
a glass-plate negative found
in the attic of a deserted house
long after. That blur at the edge
is someone who moved too fast
for the time-exposure, who leaves
the frame as fog or ectoplasm.

They all left. The glass bell
closed on an unpeopled place.
The whole is so neat you might
pick it up and shake the snow
into motion over the cemetery
whose broken-tombstone wall shows
spread palms blessing no one over and over.

Hammershøi's Rooms

Hammershøi's rooms are greatly empty.
Their emptiness is at work, hollowing further
the residences for itself.

It grows. It inhabits. It is at home.
Door upon door opens into the interior of the apartment
showing spaces on their long string.

Where Ida walks, or – more often – stands, balancing.

Here Ida sits surrounded by the resonant rooms.
She is occupied. A piece of hemming
is in her hands, she stirs the liquid
in a luminous white teacup.

The great emptiness draws in to concentrate
on this small fullness.
This presence spreads itself to contradict
apparent absence.

Then there was the bird   a robin
that a visitor to the painter heard
fluttering inside the silence
of his deep empty room.

The Painter's Wife

She senses him in the doorway of the bathroom
as she climbs into her bath, turning her face
to the watery reflection in the porcelain wall-tiles.

Very well, he may sketch her again. But she will not
pose. She will change nothing in this ritual
of letting the liquid coolness sink into her skin,

into her spirit. She slows in its snaky embrace,
its benign insinuation into the crannies of her body,
sluicing away the dry tensions. She hears his pencil's

small gushes of sound on the smooth paper,
imagines one of those sketches she never looks at.
She has heard he paints her still as a young woman,

that through their decades together he has seen
always the same body step into the bath, the same
cropped head lean on the curl of its white edge.

She exhales, lengthening in the water, letting
her weight pull her deeper, so the figure
he is drawing has more room to hang above her

in the space she does not need. Her life continues
under the images, as secret as a sea-bottom
creature that science has not yet described.

Marthe

She is there again, washing again,
slipping into the clear chilled water
of the tiger-clawed white bath
and lying there, her limbs elongated
under the surface, only her head and neck
rising into the dry;
                    though he locked the door
on her yellow bedroom when she died,
left her essence closed in the still air
of that space, where nothing but light
striped by slatted shutters moved.

Listen to the sound of water sluiced
over her skin, that echo that plays
back and forth between the tiled walls,
enlarging and enlarging the little room.

And light through alternative shutters
is caught up by the different glazes,
catches fire, kindling red and golden
from white porcelain and her wet body,
standing now, absorbed in her work
of brush on flesh, her bent head blurred.

'Still Life with a Pewter Flagon'

Barely still at all, this 'still life'.
The napkin was just flung down,
a raspberry yet rolls a little
on the pewter plate, and the light –
oh surely the light has newly brimmed
the dish, touched the flagon's round
side with a bright moon, caused
the linen's white reflection in glass
and silver, porcelain – everywhere.

Goethe defined colours as 'the deeds
and sufferings of light'. Red, indeed,
is raised here in the berries and the
almost-hidden wine, a brown-green
from the vine leaves and table cover;
but chiefly the light is itself and
about its own business – bouncing,
rebounding, exalting itself in glaze
and shine and lustre, such lustre.

The word for "beautiful" in Dutch is
schoen, also meaning "clean". And before
these objects were set up for their
portrait, there was laundering and
polishing to be done. An absent cloth
was grimed and put aside, an absent
woman breathed on the flagon's belly,
rubbed at it, breathed and rubbed...
Her life's also inherent here.

The Statues

The statues are all turned away from me
and look out to the sea. Waves break
theatrically, flinging strings of foam.
The statues do not stir. Their stone hair
hangs in corkscrews, still. Their backs
are perfect reversed triangles.
                              I walk
around them. Spray wets my hair to curl.
The statues do not stir. Hole in the centre
of each eye looks through me, past me,
at the gesturing sea. More than delight
in such waves' antics lifts the corners
of their graven lips.
                    I stand excluded.
The statues do not stir. They have stopped,
each in the process of stepping to the sea,
weight between foot and foot, a gladness
on their mouths. Unfrozen they would clap
their hands. I do not know their reasons.

Nineteen Fifty-Six

That day a whole womanhood away...
It was the year of puberty – first blood
in my bathing-suit on my birthday
beside the cold sea. A heaviness come,

the heaviness I saw in one woman
in the wall of refugees risen to sing
their anthem in the stark mansion
which housed them for that winter.

The forty-years-on perspective closes
a fist of darkness about this scene...
An invisible wind leaned on the windows,
cold climbed from sole to shin to knee

as if I were wading that Atlantic surf
I could not swim in, wadded with
cottonwool. They had known a fiercer
freezing in their own Hungarian cities

and shouldered this aside, their heads
breaking the water as they rose to sing
what was itself a sea – plummet lead
could not reach its bottom. And in pink

ballet tights and fuchsia tutu I stood
among the other Christmas entertainers,
fronting a cliff which was also liquid,
the singers wearing dissolving faces.

Despite the new breasts on my sturdy
ribcage, I was obliterated. I saw
the woman raise a mouth thirsty
for an unobtainable then settle for

drinking her own tears. I watched her
close her eyes on me, on us, to taste
their salt. Her voice with the others
built a great wave – I took its weight

on my chest... The breath knocked from us,
we could barely pipe 'God Save the Queen'
to end the ceremony. They were courteous
to those lying prostrate on their beach.

Bystanding

We have our own concerns –
as the snail on the stem
slides on its one foot upward,
despite the dragon arriving
through the adjacent trees;

we forage likewise for
what feeds our particular lives,
gathering samphire from the rock
where today a young woman
is fixed by loops of chain –

she will be gone tomorrow –
and, oh, your eyes, my love,
your eyes encounter mine
across the grassy battleground
where cliff meets forest.

That knight passing through
thinks he's a superstar,
posturing on his white horse;
we'll walk the other way,
drawing the copse around us,

and ignore the grunts and shrieks
that go on a little time
while our mouths feed on berries
and each other's tongues,
the snail slipping past us fast.

Verdure Tapestry

After the gates had closed on Adam
this is how it was in Eden. The beasts
shouldered off his chosen names
and became themselves, each distilled
to an absolute essence and frozen
in a moment of self-recognition
as they heard their own breath among leaves

and little else but leaves and breath.
The no-longer heron, slim as grass,
stood on its toes like a finger pressed
to lips, all verticals. The abada, that
had trampled its sloughed name underfoot
then slowed and stopped, was a rock
outside and within its armour plating.

The thick leaves framed them, crowded
in on them, screened them out. And
behind the succulent layers beasts
played for the first time with possibility.
So the elegant giraffe, all over dappled
with shadows of trees, put on a giant
horn, is almost unicorn in this hung Eden.

Arkadia

I have done this: emphasised the randomness
of trees by felling, planting; had islands raised
in the stream's dammed water; built temples
and aqueducts and hermitages from found fragments
of heterogeneous ruins gathered here, mortared together.

I mean to come upon it unawares, to arrive
unexpectedly at a lake where the large carp
shoulder aside the limpid surface pitted all over
with summer flies, and be surprised by the vista
crowned in the distance with a cupola's white cloud.

I shall learn from my own teaching. That island tomb
copied from Poussin's painting and incised with
'Et in Arcadia Ego' will be my school for
meditation on mortality in the approved style...
Death is here in the garden, walking on soft feet.

For when these have come to match my blueprint,
they will not stay still: blight blasts a significant
tree while another sends out shoots excessively,
growing over-heavy, drooping; in the Temple of Diana
damp blooms across the plaster and loosens stucco;

one winter of long rain has drowned an island
and altered the shape of the lake, the aqueduct
overflowed; and, going to the tomb today, I found
the body of a swan in the shallows like a soggy
tattered feathered hat gone out of fashion.

The Harpies

The harpies have smart wasp-waists;
their hats are trimmed with bones and feathers
and tilted coquettishly over a malicious eye.

In niches across the city they pose as statues,
taking the shadow within the curve of stone
for their hiding-place in broad daylight.

They watch the execution sites, where bullet-holes
in the granite have weathered under rain and
flowers are left on the pavement in twos and threes.

Their cheeks are starved. Their waists are impossibly
slender. Memorial blooms are no use as fodder
so they cruise the rubbish heaps for meat.

In the Saxon Gardens, after the lunching office girls
have left, they dispute the viands with some few
pigeons, snatching inexpertly, howling softly.

Peace does not suit them. The flame on the tomb
of the unknown soldier leaps too high,
singeing their wings as they pass in the dusk.

Yet they hang about in this city that armies
have demolished over and over. Their nostrils still
scent cordite and gunpowder in church porches.

So their anorexic feet cling to the cornices,
they press bony shoulders into the eggshell caress
of untenanted embrasures. Shabbily they endure.

Speech for Grendel's Mother

Comb my hair and braid it.
Pour water into my mouth
and I shall speak...

There was a grain, the smallest,
fell into the water, swelled there,
bobbed and floated till it came
to halt against my breastbone;
and I took it up, nurtured it
with blood from a bitten vein.

Oh my son, my son, so little then,
potato in my fist, budding,
breaking into limbs as my ichor
pumped under your skin; I made
a man-machine of you in the dark
water, all black-oiled joints.

My skin is parched. I thirst.
Splash my cheeks, wet my lips
to let the speaking come...

There, it was there, in a dry place,
alight night after night, loud
with carousing over the quiet
of black ice clenching the whole
white land; there he fought, there
he let fall his blood, our blood.

Unnatural location, made hall,
mead-hall of worked dead wood;
there, within walls, boxed in,
out of touch with ground and water,
he struggled in hot darkness,
the hewn trunks caging him.

There is fog across my eyes.
In the dim I grope with lips
and teeth, reluctant tongue...

Light dies just below the surface
of black water, and we go on down,
parting its flesh with paddled hands
or arrowed feet. The water muscles
lie to left and right, flexing,
shivering, felt as affectionate pressure.

Praise be for water sucked into
the bones of us, my son and me,
march-steppers, amphibians,
breathers of snow-melt, bog-sweat,
walkers beneath the ice and
in waterfalls' undersea continuance.

I pant. I come to it again.
Help me with attention.
Comb my very eyelashes...

Must, I must climb up, climb out
of the towering water, to stalk dry
where the killer drinks and stopper
the mead in his neck, leave him
dry, throttled, supped instead of
supping, turn that blood, take it...

Necessity, responsibility, beast's law
of tooth for tooth took hold, hauled
me there and back and into battle
on my own ground; man's law of eye
for eye took me by the hair, hauled
this head to where you hear it, here.

A Shape of Ice

Black-ice rain falling, coating everything with glass –
the road underfoot, the wall he might have clung to,
all of it slicked and frozen – freezing dark varnish
onto leaves, thin strings of winter grass, his shoes.

Arrived somehow, he let down his umbrella, and
for an infinitesimal moment there it hung –
another glass umbrella shining in the dark air
then fallen in shards and splinters around his feet.

I know what he means, having dreamed my shape
of ice, that hung like a pale smear of foam
in the darkened corridor – and generated terror...
Yet still my companion seized it by the tail

to bring it freezing inside the lighted room.
I crunched it in my teeth to share his bravado.
It had been a tiger but turned to lemon ice,
a wild thing tamed, died almost at once in the mouth.

Tiger-Taming

My small niece told me
that in his yellow toybox
the fierce tiger kept
a toy fierce tiger.

She had the same
yellow toybox.
The tiger's brilliance
roared out of it at her.

And the doll
she put to bed within –
one with her own blue eyes –
was twin for car journeys

and sitting up to eat her tea
or walks through the edges
of the nearby woods
where pigeons clattered suddenly.

She also told me
that when Goldilocks decided
she didn't want the porridge
and went next door instead,

the Three Bears rode away
on a red tricycle like hers.
We looked out of the window
and saw it parked by the gate.

Handling

'The Angel of Death turns the world this way and that,
just as men turn their money in their hands.'
PETER LAMBORN WILSON

There is lightning. I look down
to see the world frozen in its photograph.
Small houses. Small trees. Tiny mountains.
All lit up equally on all sides all at once.

Toy things. I handle them.
And the insect people are tumbled
from their homes. The mountains disintegrate
like cake icing under my thumbs.

I crush the trees. Against my will.
I am the great child who breaks
the spinning top she touches, whose
skipping rope unravels straight away.

Archangel with a Gun

In Jesuit churches like wedding-cake icing
the saints trampled down those infidels and devils,
their croziers clubs, their copes flung violently out.
How they would have liked to conscript this archangel
and set him up as St Valentine icon at the altar.

Where can we hide now – we in the world below –
when he struts in red and gold on heaven's ramparts,
the musket dangling from his fingers or aslant
on his brocaded shoulder – Uriel or Michael
armed and beetle-browed under a wide-brimmed hat?

We are ordinary as crows, our black clothes show
the real dust on them. We are fallible perhaps
and let our foreign coins fall in the collection plate
as if they were true pennies. But such a little sin,
a little little thing to bring this vengeance down!

A woman tells her beads against his drawing a bead
on her, on her knees, the rosary flowing over the back
of her hand. A penitent's pointed cap and paper tunic
are targets in the darker crowd. Millennia of practice
have made him non-pareil among sharpshooters.

God, did you know he had the gun and let him run amok
in the crowded market? The shot ones have toppled
onto boxed apples as if they were starving. The archangel
struts on their unprotesting skulls like Lucifer
in all his pride and the certainty no fall will follow.

Merely

*Angels are 'completely spiritual and no longer merely
a very fine material, fire-like and vaporous'.*
CATHOLIC ENCYCLOPAEDIA, 1967

I drain away,
thinning, thinning on the wind,
on the ground, the water.

I am the thermal shudder
of the emptiness
above hot rocks

then not even that,
no longer shimmer,
flicker, a change in the air.

I lament my substance
lost, this little death,
the sense of

heat subsiding,
gone from my centre.
Then no sense.

Chiaroscuro

On the small canal at night
water and wall are distinguished
only as matte or shiny darkness –
black light, black blotting-paper;

until after the corner is turned
and the square in the wall with
the furnace in it falls into the water
like a spinning, exploding shell:

incandescence overflowing,
white-hot light multiplying on
liquid surface and in that liquid's
quick-silver fleeting refractions.

A small man rides the flying shell,
fuels its furnace from his shovel –
wet arms flaring, slick leather apron
aflame – and is not consumed.

Madonna del Parto

(after Piero della Francesca)

This is a Turkish pavilion lined with fur or quilting,
such as are pitched for ornamental battles, plays
of war with pennants gay in the wind and armour
polished into dazzle on the backcloth of greensward.

I wait here, enclosed and enclosing. In a sense,
I am a Turkish pavilion lined with quilting,
set up for a battle upon a daisied field.
We are arrayed alike: the tent slit open,
my dress seams cut in three places just the same.

Behold the scene. Small angels here reveal it.
Nothing is happening yet everything occurs.
The bones are building that shall break in battle,
break down inside the tomb then build again.
The pavilion breathes in a balmy wind. I feel
my breath and his lift underneath my hand.

Couvade

The whole convent shares a kind of pregnancy:
delicate-bellied, we linger under high grilles,
bathing our suppressed breasts in falling light;
stare fixedly through stone to where
the invisible arriving road must surely be.

Master Erhart has carved us a Christ-child.
We wait for him calm as Mary when the angel
winged away from her, his elevating feet
agitating with their wind a few stray hairs
about her temples: annunciation accomplished.

Look at him:
life-sized, exact;
navel like a nail-head,
sex like a curved shell;
he flexes at hip and knee,
shoulder and elbow and neck.

In turn we take him
to these virgin breasts
weighed flat by scapulars;
he lies some time on every lap –
dressed afresh by each of us,
flushed, faintly smiling.

If he should come alive, if he should come alive
from all the hands laid warm on him. Think of it:
flesh other than our own under our glad fingers,
the strange skin answering with temperature and
pressure, then some small stirring – a hair, a lip.

Mary had a son as well as saviour. There were days
he was simply child – fretful at first teeth, giddy
with turning on himself like a top in the garden...
We roll the god-doll in our palms. His frock in the wind
bells out. His feet underneath it could be running.

Flight

No rest. Fleeing to his father
to escape his mother's anger,
he was forestalled among
the green hedges steamy with
high summer's small insects.

Astride the gate, he looked down
on the basking adder, olive
and thick-bodied where his foot
was about to fall. Panting already,
he pulled back, jumped down, ran on

a longer way through the rooms
of the empty manor's gardens,
all that uniform flat green
that comes just before the autumn's
variations, fagged out, dusty.

No rest. Wrecked for a moment
against his father's body, starting
to tell the viper, he was driven
off again. Three hornets hung
in the air above the other's head,

huger than wasp queens, red and
yellow striped. All his taught fears
caught in his breathless mouth,
he fled anew through the green
humming garden maze, without

object now, any hope of rest
surrendered, flight for its own sake
driving the pump of his lungs,
the pistons of his running legs,
on and on in a blur of wings.

Swaddled

Swaying still on the hook
after the hurried act of hanging,
the swaddled child looks down,
mild-eyed, on the passage-room

of dark-brown panels and a plain chair
slightly skewed. Her heart ticks slow
and breathing does not stir her bandages.
Her limbs are shut away

in a coffin-outline bundle.
Light walks upon the linen.
The nurse has left her here, for safety
for a second. Chrysalis in a cobweb.

Pyramid

Museum. Knitting. Ancient Egyptians.
Old pullovers unravelled and washed
in skeins to start with once again.
'I shall knit myself a sarcophagus.'

It used to be that youths of the Red Army,
off duty occupying this satellite state,
trooped through the room because
there was nowhere else to go. They went.

Now hardly anybody comes in their place.
The old woman sits and knits and supervises
the cats in bandages and viscera in jars,
the mummy-cases in ranks up on end.

She feels very old in their way – near eternal.
Not bones aching or bones thinning, but
the bones preserved, correctly paralleled,
wrapped, cushioned and anointed, sweet.

Her thin white fingers play about the wool.
She knits them up in it, the long-agos,
then neat as ninepins they are laid aside
in rows within the pyramid of herself.

Though she tells them over, plain and purl,
where they're piled against oblivion –
lives made, unravelled, made again,
pullover sarcophagi cramming the chambers.

'My Mother Had a Maid Called Barbary...'

A Barbary horse, a Berber woman, Barbara of the tower
with three windows for the Trinity... a maid going
about her business with generally downcast eyes.
Secret: the veiled face, foreign steed, steeple of stone.

She keeps her counsel, unfolding the linen underclothing
and laying it ready, mending rent silk, licking
the end of the thread to slick it for the needle,
embroidering eyelet holes at the neck of a nightgown.

Look through them at evening into a bedroom
made small by their circumference, everything
miniaturised; the fine lawn for a shroud across
the features, mouth throbbing like a fontanelle.

Outside a horse's shoes ring hollow on the cobbles,
swelling the round black emptiness of the night.
Still, at the window, its lace over her face, she sees
only the tremor of shadows, waves of the lack of light.

They lap the tower that is herself, the contained woman
upright in the room, waiting for her role to come to her
in the shape of a lady to be clothed, unclothed.
In the meantime she is this castle, dark-besieged.

She keeps her counsel. Only within, that voice
that cries *willow, willow, willow* to her head,
relentless as the hooves of galloping horses never
passing by. Her downcast eye beholds the tumult.

Translation

White-hot pearls, incandescent from her desire,
a nose-ring become like heated wire for putting out
of eyes, bangles in glass that is the shimmer above
an open fire – she casts them from her, down onto
the unvisited bed of leaves, over the peacock's head
on the high terrace she looks out from, unrequited.

One language. She has not the abundant tropical jewels
festooning a near-naked body to tell back her longing.
Though she partly understands. In the big frost,
in the street, she tore the gilt hoops from her ears
when their temperature plummeted far below her own,
searing flesh in their ardent freezing. This translation.

The Appalling Jasmine

When she was sick he sent her flowering jasmine –
white stars spare in a dark-green polished sky.

She smelt nothing, the whole flocked world
neutral as blotting paper wadded against her nose;
but she knew what sweetness waited for her
in the star flowers – honey on honey, almost cloying.

She was not sure she could face that scent
fighting its way to her through the fluffed layers
that swathed her whole head, the pillow as helmet.
She had fended off sweetness a long time now.

And what would come with all the sugar
flooding her nostrils and laid down on her tongue?
Memories put by like linen in a hope chest –
with dried lavender between the sheets, rose petals,
orris root; for years she had refused to lift the lid.

So this was appalling jasmine, looming like a threat
above her bed, a dark-green leaning shape with
arms and fingers. What was he about who had sent
this box of sweets to rouse her into life again
when she thought she was put by, shelved and dry?

Bedsides

1

I stood by their bedside, small in the dark,
my chin at blanket level. 'There's a bubble
in my throat.'
           'Then swallow it,' she said
out of the dim pillows.
               'If I swallow it,
will I die?' die, die. The fear of death was strong
in the quiet room in the house with water
all around it. I felt beset by earthquakes,
seeing our home each night slip through a slot
in the ground that closed again after that morsel.

Our upper floor had listed from the level
like a boat, so that the furniture fetched up
against one wall no matter how they tried
to rearrange it.
           'There's a bubble in my throat.'
You could drown with a line of such balls of breath
drifting upwards from your mouth through the wet.
'Then swallow it,' she said, patient but
weary of this old ritual.
             'Will I die? Will I die?'
I asked her the question night after night. 'No,'
she replied again. I believed it and could sleep.

2

I stood at her bedside, feeling tall as a gantry
over that unconsciousness in a sea of white –
sheets, pillow, blankets, bandage, hospital walls
dazzling like sun on water.
             She had drowned
overnight in her own blood. The bubble
that was the aneurysm had swelled and thinned
and burst within her brain. A vein of her head
had opened like an earthquake fissure
and swallowed her house whole.

                              I could not say
she would not die. She was dying already
between the wrung-out sheets, her breaths
drawn rasping over gravel, and so slow
that life stopped in her throat after each one.

I turned to the window where it was bright day
and glass cooled my forehead.
                              There was no
further comfort. That was gone with the voice
out of the earlier darkness that told me the way
to get to sleep again.
                              All the words had changed.
From 'bubble' and 'swallow' innocence had fled;
'throat' was the tunnel through which her death
was crawling, while I stood by unable to say 'No'.

Language

In these photographs the dead soldiers
have all the vulnerability of children
asleep in postures of abandonment.
Arms thrown wide. Legs sprawled.

Until their time lays claim to them.
This is December 1942.
It is the Russian Front.
These are German corpses.

So the picture of this youth
whose head is forced to crook
against the sheer side of an open grave,
whose shirt is undone at his throat,
whose tunic is unbuttoned
under a powdering of light-coloured earth
or snow

is labelled
'*Lebensraum* for one more Nazi'.

This other spread-eagled face down,
a dark shape in his winter padding,
bears a thin line of brilliant fire
along one arm and
working on his back.

His caption reads: 'The enemy:
one of the Fascist robbers is halted,
and on his tank the flame springs up
that will burn him and all his kind.'

Another Language

This object, this vessel
curving upward from a flattened circle base,
with a handle that accommodates a couple
of fingers, a finger and a thumb –

we have agreed to call it 'cup'
all of us using this language. This is arbitrary.
The 'cupping' of hands derives from such a vessel,
is metaphor by consensus.

In the camps it was agreed
that the Jews should be known as 'logs of wood'.
So much simpler then to stack their inanimation,
to lop their limbs for kindling.

Though another language
was whispered in the dark between the shelves
of bed-planks – nicknames, pet names, patronymics –
logs bursting into leaf.

Grandmother, after her stroke,
called every cup a 'saucer', a knife a 'fork',
we learned to take each 'no' she said for 'yes'.
All her words were reversals

of the expected ones.
How surprisingly easy it was in this dark wood
to navigate by their shadows instead of the trees,
to come to a new consensus.

This cup is very slippery,
tugging away from two fingers and a thumb.
It may be a trick of the senses or a ghost story,
it may be a saucer after all.

Ghosts

Solomon Anski, travelling in Galicia,
found shadow communities of Jews,
made ghostly by persecution.
He wrote of how those people
hovered in other, unknown worlds,
their faces full of secrets.

The gatehouse of Vilna ghetto
is a shadow on the ground,
a shape of cobbles laid in concentric circles.
My foot did not feel its difference
from Gaono Street's stones set in ranks
when I came down the hill to that place.

There were some trees, a little grass,
a space to park a car or two.
The slope stopped at a junction,
and we crossed the road and went on
into the university district, stepping upon
the round flat island and off again unthinking.

Anski brought back a dybbuk,
the unknown world made manifest
in an extra voice from a young girl's throat,
the additional male curled inside the woman.
He built a gatehouse of words around it,
to domicile the secret on the real ground.

Reaped

But to make hay in Birkenau
amid the dreadful regular plantation
of brick chimneys to the horizon...

I have taken for granted
the wholesomeness of hay, its sweetness
in stacks and haycocks. The bucolic scene.

The unmanned guard-towers look down
on spread hay. The wire marks off
huge rectangles of fresh-reaped ground.

All manner of scythes have done their work,
nothing standing but obsolete chimneys...
And on the road a rabbit's compressed corpse.

Century

Photographs

1

That light and time could make this picture!
My eyes flinch, but still the men stand in rows,
naked and skeletal, their heads shaven.

I turn the page. Turn back.
Something insists that I should look at this
vertical patterning of shades of grey. A bad photograph –
in all senses. Over-exposed and over-exposed.

Wherever this is from – Auschwitz or Dachau or
Sachsenhausen, Treblinka – its object is humiliation.
Stripped of even the hairs of their heads, they stand –
naked, forked creatures, pale misshapen roots.

And to look at it, I have to take a place
at the photographer's shoulder. I am opposite their shame.
Complicit, through my looking, in the taking
(oh, it is *taking*) of the picture. I turn the page.

Turn back. To find their faces –
which, in the flare of too much light on flesh,
are vestiges. In bleached-out wedges four smudges
of eyes and nose and mouth. Holes poked in dough
by a child's fingers. My eyes flinch.

There is no way of ending this description.
Looker and looked-at continue in their cage, continue.
How can I see with other than this dreadful
camera's vision? Impossible space to cross.

2

Only a camera ever saw this. Nobody stood behind it.
Nobody bent and squinted through the viewfinder,
a black cloth flung over his head.
I am at no one's elbow when I look.

And this, in my hand, is not even a photograph
in the usual sense. It's further mediated.
A smudged newspaper picture of
a second from the television screen.
The best that could be done in the situation –
indistinct, grainy, and momentous.

To one side a dark-grey contraption – gantry,
scaffolding? Then, half-fused with it,
a slightly lighter grey, a frogman figure –
squat, bulked-out, visored. Behind, the horizon
bright as a knife blade with the sun in it.

Something is frozen in commemoration
that took its meaning only from a movement,
a small transfer of weight.
I remember it on the television screen,
at 3.56 in the morning, London time.

His helmet and shoulders square to the unmanned camera,
the figure in the diving suit tilted,
taking one step onto the Moon.

Here it is not at all. This picture is an icon,
no more than representative, symbolic;
the step itself so hugely far away – although I saw it.

Stars

   1

How long does it take for the light of the Moon
to reach us? How long for the moon-rocket's
pinprick of reflected dazzle to fall again to Earth?

Apollo 13, crippled by an explosion that perhaps
a meteorite caused, was a ship of the old dispensation,
navigating by the stars in a dearth of light and
air and drinking-water. Three men pitted against
a universe of galaxies, a radiant velvet ocean.

The shine of astronauts moon-walking.
Lit cylinders in a fuzz of sun off rock
before the sharp cut-off of the horizon,
brilliance into black, abyss on its back.

Their craft rotated to mitigate a Sun
unfiltered by the atmosphere of clouds and breath.
It rose over and over each day in their sky,
where else there was neither up nor down –
excess of water stayed on the spoon, a glittering dome.

I thought the world had stretched in their direction,
the bag of consciousness pulled out to include
the Moon and more. I walked on little streets,
travelled on Tube trains smaller than worms in the soil,
while above me the sky flowered higher and huger.

2

When they were clothed, it was to put on
the yellow star. Six-pointed, sickly, Judas Iscariot
coloured. David's signet abased, abused.

These were stars brought down from the heavens
into an under-night, another kind of darkness
condensed in a stifling place. Strait as an unlit cellar.

They had relative brightness only in the sense
of pyres, fired houses. He said that when he donned one,
'it burned through my clothes, burned deep into my heart'.

This, irrecusably, has become the truth of stars –
that they can be used this way, as plague signs.
At the top of the Christmas tree the foil star tarnishes,
begins to show its invisible-ink inscription – 'Jude'.
How can she ever dress in star-print cotton?

The old Jew in his gaberdine, with the rough-cut
yellow patch sewn to his back at its six points,
is straightening from his bent position.
I see this rear view clear, without before or after.
The image, at its edges, trails off into cloud.

Space holds it and the place at the back of my eyes.
A picture that light in every sense has drained from,
but that time retains – so the looking must continue...

Iconography

I suppose it was a Gothic face: the long upper lip,
the prominent cheekbones, the sense of excess flesh
burned away (perhaps by the heat of candle flames)
until all that remained were lines – of jawbones, brow,
the teeth within the slightly-open downturned mouth.

To speak of this face is to mean both the wooden Christs
and also the living beggar woman in the portico
of St Anne's, her folded long bones hugging the cold
marble floor, snuggling the stone doorframe.
Her lids were tight veils on the globes of her eyes.

All three faces contained themselves, held their suffering
as if in translucent alabaster vases. Queen Jadwiga's
black Christ refused to present his passion to an onlooker,
but gazed within, conserving it for himself.
Likewise the museum's scourged Christ, absorbed

in his troubled private gravity. And the woman
looked nowhere, asked nothing, was no more
than illustrative caryatid to the plastic box
on the plinth above her. Yet these faces were full vessels...
What was not contained, but spilled; what sloshed

endlessly, gathered into waves, leaned on and eroded
walls and dykes: was the lost face of the child
whose intricately-knitted tiny silk undervest
reposed with other children's clothing in a glass case
at Auschwitz, its only symbol this shed wrapping.

Afterlives

Archaeology

Her skull is stuffed with marmot hair and grass.
The little marmot memory sneaked off into the grass
and could not be tracked for the wind's muddling.

The words are like teeth scattered on the ground,
or the loosened teeth that fall from her lifted skull
are like words she would have spoken, protesting.

But her silk blouse is preserved, a hunk of mutton
beside the coffin, gold leaf unseated from wooden jewels.
These cup her, make a vessel in which the drink has dried.

Her tale is a fume momentarily tasted on the roof
of the mouth as they open the tomb. Scheherazade
she is, beginning a new instalment of compacted air.

Cryonics

Nothing came with him into this sterile chamber.
The taste of his world was air-locked outside
the door. He is more naked than anything alive.

His head is everything, meant to engender incarnation,
flesh put on downwards from the neck into that space
his skull trails now like a comet its transparent tail.

His brain is a soft fossil awaiting the unfreezing
to spread and fatten like dried fungus water-filling.
The memory has slept four hundred years unkissed.

But it's not that story so far as I know. So far
there is no story. He's a stopped clock, a stalled
car, mechanism in suspension, his menders unborn.

The Dry Mermaid

Dumb as a cliff, as rock bottom;
quiet as weed and beach sand and the water in a pool,
her tongue lies salty in her mouth
and swells with the tide at the full and the dark
of the moon seen through a latticed window
or between two chimneys.

The Earth's shadow stains that luminous satellite;
the land leaves its marks on her fingers,
scrapes the scales from her grounded tail forever
and weights her like a sack with gravity
that the sea lifts off its fishes
and casts back again on the shore.

The Building

What I thought was a truly concrete building,
solid and foursquare and elephant dull grey,
now lurches like a boat caught broadsides
by sudden wind; and what I feel is surely
mal de mer, sick judder homing under my ribs.

These yellow machines on caterpillar tracks,
with great hinged arms and jagged jaws,
are breaking the ground before the building.
They whine and turn and throb, restless with
appetite like sharks around one bleeding.

And we at the top of the building resemble
Lear's Gloucester on a cliff without his eyes.
Below and out of sight our rock is undermined
by this sea's grinding, concaves are excavated
in perpendiculars, the tempest lifts towards us.

When I needed to set it aside, it was my way
to shrink the building lodged behind my eyes.
I'd walk around it first, getting its measure –
the elephant-grey solidity, the foursquare bulk –
then render it down to dolls' house size and heft

and summon the hot-air balloon that would
take it up, fitted neatly inside the wicker cradle.
It would rise before my eyes as in a lift shaft
until I could block it out with one thumbnail
and set it drifting over the sea to nothing.

What was left behind was a map of stained
concrete in the shape of the abducted building.
I would walk there too, willing weeds to erupt
through the cracks and the rain's slow erosion;
then abandon the meaningless site to crows.

Lesson

The wind presses its multiple mouths
against the glass of the several windows –
all closed, but still the blinds flap and clatter.
I have lived this on so many mornings.
The air in the classroom is cold as water,
heaps on my knees underneath the desk.
Wind catcalls outside, drowning our voices –
though today there's a certain appropriateness:
we are on the heath with the Fool and Lear.
'Blow winds and crack your cheeks!'

It's not getting through to them:
they read the words aloud like people afraid
of what phrases might do – slip out of their mouths
like soap in the bath escaping the clutching hand;
turn in the water to other things, as Japanese
paper flowers have. And I love it so. 'Listen,'
I say, 'to that flat vowel in "strike" then
hear the fatness of the word "rotundity".'
They return my lifted gaze fishily, blankly,
consigning such eccentric ears to me alone.

The gulls are roller-coastering outside the window,
one flies into the gale but does not progress,
stays a long time in one spot in the air.
I could see that bird as metaphor for myself,
but it's melodramatic; what's going on has
a weekliness (at least) I should be used to.
I can always get their attention explaining
codpieces; and anyway the seconds pass, ticking
like sudden rain thrown against the panes
that makes them look up as if called outside.

Sarah Bernhardt's Wooden Leg

Sarah Bernhardt had a wooden leg.
I don't know why this was or when she got it,
but today, going barefoot at home for the first time
after winter, I think of that leg on the Paris cobbles.
A wooden foot is all heel on the ice.

I am afraid of ice on the ground.
I wait to fall with every step, to fall and fall again
over and over, for breakages and spillages and
my own wooden leg to replace the flesh-and-blood one
shattered into five on the ice.

I expect those falls to last as long
as though I were setting out across a frozen lake
and not a pavement, as though I could crash
not onto ice but through it, into the near-zero water,
and clutch up the wooden leg like a saving spar.

So I take tiny steps like a pony's,
act out my feet as Chinese, bound and shrunk.
I carry my own small skating rink beneath each shoe,
feel the world turn away from underneath my heel,
its curvature kick-started.

I cannot trust myself to move,
each entire foot thus reduced to a mere high heel.
I am Sarah Bernhardt fitted with her wooden leg,
facing the horror of Parisian ice-slicked cobbles.
And I'd rather be dead – like she is after all.

Heart's Delight

Why did I never find out Heart's Delight
where the signpost pointed? I remember saying,
'How could it possibly live up to that name?'
and staying put at the bottom of the valley
while others took the track up the flank of the hill.

This is no metaphor. The fingerpost was real,
down by the river where a plague of caterpillars
had shredded the leaves of the trees then hung
on threads below. A starting point silent except
for water. Sinisterly unlikely to delight a heart.

When the others came back down the hill they said,
'It was only a pub.' But that is not the issue.
That someone who as a girl had run in joy
up any slope, expecting glory on the crest of it,
should pass up the promise of 'Heart's Delight'...

this is growing old the Gorgon's way, petrifaction
among the river boulders, with caterpillars dangling.

Return

I've come back from under the hill,
though I was paramour of the Lord there,
and he was fine in green clothing,
his profile like a blade by candlelight.

I've arrived to find my children grown
and gone, the apple-pip I planted
at the gate stretched to a tree bearing
its crop of apples how green in the air.

Nobody knows me, and no wonder.
I've looked in the glass and since
I crossed the threshhold a lock of hair
has turned white at my temple.

Otherwise I'm the woman who stepped
through the door in the hill and into
the arm of that tall Lord looking
down on me, his eyes two further caves.

It would seem to have been a dream
had the world not grown old without me.
The bookworm has eaten a road
right through my shelf of stories.

Diptych

1

There's a manikin in my head.
He approves of me, he adores me without my asking
saying he does, he does.

He is beautiful.
My mind grooms his cheekbones,
polishing them with reiteration soft as silk handkerchiefs.

But what he really approves
is the girl inside my brain
whose grace is my life's learning fossilised into youth.

They kiss, she rests against his chest.
They express themselves through all the familiar postures,
motions of mouth and hand.

I am less and less at home within my skull.
My foot won't fit the fosil slipper
that's youth and beauty.

My manikin will grow sick of this stabling too,
of reiteration, treasuring
into some Dorian Gray without the mitigating picture.

2

'Look on this picture' and on this
that Giovanni di Paolo painted –
John the Baptist goes forth twice over, dressed in pink.

He's beautiful in fifteenth-century fashion,
with golden curls
and profile sharp incised on the coin of his halo.

He has Dick Whittington's bundle-on-a-stick
but small as a coin-purse,
and jauntily, in duplicate, he 'retires to the desert'.

Get away into the wilderness, manikin of mine.
Do as di Paolo's storyboard suggests –
follow the grey-green road.

On the edge of sight in this strip-cartoon painting
the horizon curves like the world
breeding clouds.

And I can dress up in pink without your adoration,
step out as your twin by myself,
leaving that girl in her cold stone shoes behind.